Chocolate Box

Chocolate Box

Indulge in the finest chocolate recipes
for serious chocolate lovers

This edition published in 2010
LOVE FOOD is an imprint of Parragon Books Ltd

Parragon
Queen Street House
4 Queen Street
Bath BA1 1HE, UK

ISBN: 978-1-4454-0868-2

Printed in China

Design by Fiona Roberts
Photography by Mike Cooper
Home economy by Sumi Glass and Lincoln Jefferson
Introduction by Linda Doeser

Notes for the Reader
This book uses both metric and imperial measurements. Follow the same units of measurement
throughout; do not mix metric and imperial. All spoon measurements are level: teaspoons are assumed
to be 5 ml, and tablespoons are assumed to be 15 ml.

Unless otherwise stated, milk is assumed to be full fat, eggs and individual vegetables are medium,
and pepper is freshly ground black pepper.

The times given are an approximate guide only. Preparation times differ according to the techniques
used by different people and the cooking times may also vary from those given.
Optional ingredients, variations or serving suggestions have not been included in the calculations.

Recipes using raw or very lightly cooked eggs should be avoided by infants, the elderly, pregnant
women, convalescents and anyone suffering from an illness. Pregnant and breastfeeding women are
advised to avoid eating peanuts and peanut products.

Sufferers from nut allergies should be aware that some of the ready-made ingredients used in the
recipes in this book may contain nuts. Always check the packaging before use.

Contents

Introduction 6

Chocolate Heaven 10

Baked to Perfection 52

Crumbly Cookies & Heavenly Bites 98

Cool Chocolate 134

Little Treats & Luxury Drinks 180

Index 224

Introduction

'Blissful', 'heavenly', 'divine' or even 'to die for' – words of praise we immediately associate with this

magical foodstuff. However, chocoholics of the twenty-first century are far from the first people to regard

this unique, indulgent treat as precious and associate it with paradise. In the eighteenth century, the

Swedish botanist Carolus Linnaeus, who devised a scientific system for classifying plants, named the

cacao bush from which chocolate is produced *Theobroma* – food of the gods. Yet cocoa beans had been

highly valued by the native people of Central and South America centuries before any European landed on

its shores.

The Maya not only ate the sun-dried beans, probably ground to a paste and possibly mixed with water,

but cultivated the bushes on which they grew. Depictions of the god *Ek-chuah* processing cocoa still

exist today and it is also known that the Maya used the beans as a form of currency for trade before their

civilisation died out in circa 900 AD. Further north in what is now Mexico, the Toltec people also valued the

sun-dried beans and when they were conquered by the Aztec in 1325, cocoa beans became the currency of

the new empire.

The World's Favourite Confectionery

The chocolate of today is very different from that of pre-Columbian America. The Aztecs had discovered that, if the beans fermented before they dried in the sun, they had a less bitter flavour. They also developed techniques for crushing, roasting, grinding and mixing the fat-rich cocoa paste with cold water. Chocolate was now a drink, served to kings and princes in gold cups.

In the sixteenth century, the Spanish conquistadors began to flavour the drink with spices from Spain and regarded it as a stimulant that improved the endurance of soldiers. It then became fashionable in Spain itself and its Caribbean colonies, but nowhere else, until the Italians became aware of it 100 years later and began to import cocoa beans. From there the fame of this now hot rather than cold drink, sometimes made with milk, spread throughout Europe. Fashionable chocolate houses appeared in all the major cities from Vienna to London and poems were written in praise of this elixir.

The transformation from drink to confectionery could not begin until the dawn of the Machine Age. Separating out the cocoa butter was the first stage in 1828, patented by Dutchman C. J. van Houten, and other developments followed, but it was Swiss confectioners who produced the first real 'eating' chocolate.

Types of Chocolate

The quality of chocolate depends on the quality of the raw ingredients and on the manufacturing process. As a general rule, the higher the percentage of cocoa butter, the better the flavour and texture of the product – and the higher the price. Good chocolate should be even in texture with no grains or specks and should have a distinctive chocolate taste rather than a flavour of cocoa. It should melt on the tongue and not feel sticky or greasy. With the exception of couverture (see below), all types of chocolate are made in varying quality.

* Milk chocolate has added milk solids, usually about 14 per cent, and milk fats. It is quite sweet with up to 55 per cent sugar and is light brown in colour.

* Plain chocolate is dark brown and only lightly sweetened.

* Dark chocolate is very dark, sometimes almost black, and is very lightly sweetened.

* Couverture is always high-quality plain or dark chocolate designed for cooking, icing and making confectionery. It has a high percentage of cocoa butter, which makes it very workable, but it must be tempered before use. This involves heating and cooling to specified temperatures and then working the chocolate with a metal spatula.

* White chocolate is not strictly chocolate because it is made from cocoa butter but contains no cocoa solids. It is more accurately known as white confectionery coating, but you are unlikely to see it advertised in this way on supermarket shelves.

* Chocolate-flavoured cake covering has a high proportion of vegetable fat and is low in cocoa butter. It melts easily and is low in price, but the flavour is poor and it is not recommended for the recipes in this book.

* Cocoa powder is usually unsweetened and is widely used in baking. Drinking chocolate is not a substitute because it has a much milder flavour and contains sugar.

Chocolate Heaven

Chocolate Fudge Cake

SERVES 8

To make the icing, put the chocolate, sugar, butter, evaporated milk and vanilla essence in a heavy-based saucepan. Heat gently, stirring constantly, until melted. Pour into a bowl and leave to cool. Cover with clingfilm and leave to chill for 1 hour, or until spreadable. Preheat the oven to 180°C/350°F/Gas Mark 4. Grease and line two 20-cm/8-inch cake tins.

To make the cake, put the butter and sugar in a bowl and beat until light and fluffy. Gradually beat in the eggs. Stir in the syrup and ground almonds. Sift the flour, salt and cocoa into a bowl, then fold into the mixture. Add a little water if necessary to make a dropping consistency. Spoon the mixture into the prepared tins and bake in the oven for 30–35 minutes, until springy to the touch and a skewer, inserted into the centre, comes out clean.

Remove the cakes from the oven, leave in their tins for 5 minutes, then turn out on to wire racks to cool. When the cakes are completely cold, sandwich them together with half of the icing. Spread the remaining icing over the top and sides of the cake, swirling it to give a frosted appearance.

175 g/6 oz butter, unsalted for preference, softened, plus extra for greasing
175 g/6 oz caster sugar
3 eggs, beaten
3 tbsp golden syrup
3 tbsp ground almonds
225 g/8 oz self-raising flour
pinch of salt
40 g/1$\frac{1}{2}$ oz cocoa powder

ICING
225 g/8 oz plain chocolate, broken into pieces
100 g/3$\frac{1}{2}$ oz dark muscovado sugar
225 g/8 oz butter, unsalted for preference, diced
5 tbsp evaporated milk
$\frac{1}{2}$ tsp vanilla essence

Chocolate Ganache Cake

SERVES 10

Preheat the oven to 180°C/350°F/Gas Mark 4. Lightly grease and line a 20-cm/8-inch springform cake tin. Beat the butter and sugar until light and fluffy. Gradually add the eggs, beating well after each addition. Sift the flour and cocoa together. Fold into the cake mixture. Fold in the melted chocolate.

Pour into the prepared tin and smooth the top. Bake in the preheated oven for 40 minutes, or until springy to the touch. Leave the cake to cool for 5 minutes in the tin, then turn out on to a wire rack and leave to cool completely. Cut the cake into 2 layers.

To make the ganache, place the cream in a saucepan and bring to the boil, stirring. Add the chocolate and stir until melted. Pour into a bowl, cool, then chill for 2 hours, or until set and firm. Whisk the mixture until light and fluffy.

Reserve one-third of the ganache. Use the remaining ganache to sandwich the cake together and spread over the top and sides of the cake.

Melt the cake covering and spread it over a large sheet of baking paper. Leave to cool until just set. Cut into strips a little wider than the height of the cake. Place the strips around the edge of the cake, overlapping them slightly.

Pipe the reserved ganache in tear drops or shells to cover the top of the cake. Leave to chill for 1 hour.

175 g/6 oz butter, plus extra
    for greasing
175 g/6 oz caster sugar
4 eggs, beaten lightly
250 g/9 oz self-raising flour
1 tbsp cocoa powder
50 g/1¾ oz plain chocolate,
    melted
200 g/7 oz chocolate-flavoured
    cake covering

GANACHE
450 ml/16 fl oz cream
375 g/13 oz plain chocolate,
    broken into pieces

Chocolate Truffle Torte

SERVES 10

Preheat the oven to 220°C/425°F/Gas Mark 7. Grease and line a 23-cm/9-inch springform cake tin. Put the sugar and eggs in a heatproof bowl set over a saucepan of gently simmering water. Whisk together until pale and resembling the texture of mousse. Sift in the flour and cocoa and fold gently into the mixture. Pour into the prepared tin and bake in the oven for 7–10 minutes, or until risen and firm to the touch.

Transfer to a wire rack to cool. Wash and dry the tin and replace the cooled cake in the tin. Mix together the coffee and brandy and brush over the cake. To make the truffle filling, put the cream in a bowl and whisk until just holding very soft peaks. Put the chocolate in a heatproof bowl set over a saucepan of gently simmering water until melted. Carefully fold the cooled melted chocolate into the cream. Pour the chocolate mixture over the sponge. Chill until set.

To decorate the torte, sift cocoa over the top and remove carefully from the tin. Using strips of card or greaseproof paper, sift bands of icing sugar over the torte to create a striped pattern. Cut into slices with a hot knife, to serve.

SPONGE
butter, for greasing
50 g/1¾ oz caster sugar
2 eggs
40 g/1¼ oz plain flour
25 g/1 oz cocoa powder
4 tbsp strong black coffee
2 tbsp brandy

TRUFFLE FILLING
600 ml/1 pint whipping cream
425 g/15 oz plain chocolate,
  broken into pieces

TO DECORATE
cocoa powder
icing sugar

Chocolate Cake with Syrup

SERVES 12

Preheat the oven to 190°C/375°F/Gas Mark 5. Grease and line a deep 20-cm/8-inch round cake tin. Place the chocolate, butter and coffee in a heatproof bowl and set over a saucepan of gently simmering water until melted. Stir to blend, then remove from the heat and leave to cool slightly.

Place the whole eggs, egg yolks and sugar in a separate bowl and whisk together until thick and pale. Sift the flour and cinnamon over the egg mixture. Add the almonds and the chocolate mixture and fold in carefully. Spoon the mixture into the prepared tin. Bake in the preheated oven for 35 minutes, or until the tip of a knife inserted into the centre comes out clean. Leave to cool slightly before turning out on to a serving plate.

Meanwhile, make the syrup. Place the coffee, sugar and cinnamon stick in a heavy based saucepan and heat gently, stirring, until the sugar has dissolved. Increase the heat and boil for 5 minutes, or until reduced and thickened slightly. Keep warm. Pierce the surface of the cake with a cocktail stick, then drizzle over half the coffee syrup. Decorate with chocolate-covered coffee beans and serve, cut into wedges, with the remaining coffee syrup.

115 g/4 oz butter, plus extra
  for greasing
225 g/8 oz plain chocolate,
  broken into pieces
1 tbsp strong black coffee
4 large eggs
2 egg yolks
115 g/4 oz caster sugar
40 g/1½ oz plain flour
2 tsp ground cinnamon
85 g/3 oz ground almonds
chocolate-covered coffee beans,
  to decorate

SYRUP
300 ml/10 fl oz strong black
  coffee
115 g/4 oz caster sugar
1 cinnamon stick

Marble Cake

SERVES 10

Preheat the oven to 180°C/350°F/Gas Mark 4. Grease a 1.7-litre/3-pint ring mould. Put the chocolate and coffee in a heatproof bowl set over a saucepan of gently simmering water. Heat until melted. Leave to cool. Sift the flour and baking powder into a bowl. Add the butter, sugar, eggs, ground almonds and milk. Beat well until smooth.

Transfer one half of the mixture to another bowl and stir in the vanilla essence. Stir the cooled soft chocolate into the other half of the mixture. Place spoonfuls of the 2 mixtures alternately into the ring mould, then drag a skewer through to create a marbled effect. Smooth the top. Bake in the preheated oven for 50–60 minutes, until risen and a skewer, inserted into the centre, comes out clean. Leave in the mould for 5 minutes, then turn out on to a wire rack to cool.

To make the icing, put the chocolate, butter and water into a heatproof bowl set over a saucepan of simmering water. Heat until melted. Stir and pour over the cake, working quickly to coat the top and sides. Leave to set before serving.

225 g/8 oz butter, softened, plus
   extra for greasing
55 g/2 oz plain chocolate, broken
   into pieces
1 tbsp strong black coffee
280 g/10 oz self-raising flour
1 tsp baking powder
225 g/8 oz caster sugar
4 eggs, beaten
50 g/1¾ oz ground almonds
2 tbsp milk
1 tsp vanilla essence

ICING
125 g/4½ oz plain chocolate,
   broken into pieces
2 tbsp butter
2 tbsp water

Mocha Layer Cake

SERVES 8

Preheat the oven to 180°C/350°F/Gas Mark 4. Lightly grease three 18-cm/ 7-inch sandwich tins.

Sift the flour, baking powder and cocoa into a large mixing bowl. Stir in the sugar. Make a well in the centre and stir in the eggs, syrup, oil and milk. Beat with a wooden spoon, gradually mixing in the dry ingredients to make a smooth mixture. Divide the mixture between the prepared tins.

Bake in the preheated oven for 35–45 minutes, or until springy to the touch. Leave the cakes to cool in their tins for 5 minutes, then turn out on to a wire rack to cool completely.

To make the filling, dissolve the instant coffee in the boiling water and place in a bowl with the cream and icing sugar. Whip until the cream is just holding its shape. Use half of the cream to sandwich the 3 cakes together. Spread the remaining cream over the top and sides of the cake. Lightly press the chocolate shavings into the cream around the edge of the cake.

Transfer to a serving plate. Lay the caraque over the top of the cake. Cut a few thin strips of baking paper and place on top of the caraque. Dust lightly with icing sugar, then carefully remove the paper. Serve.

butter, for greasing
250 g/9 oz self-raising flour
1/4 tsp baking powder
4 tbsp cocoa powder
115 g/4 oz caster sugar
2 eggs
2 tbsp golden syrup
150 ml/5 fl oz sunflower oil
150 ml/5 fl oz milk

FILLING
1 tsp instant coffee powder
1 tbsp boiling water
300 ml/10 fl oz double cream
2 tbsp icing sugar

TO DECORATE
50 g/1 3/4 oz chocolate shavings
marbled chocolate caraque
icing sugar, for dusting

Chocolate Madeira Cake

SERVES 8–10

Preheat the oven to 180°C/350°F/Gas Mark 4. Lightly oil and line an 18-cm/7-inch cake tin with non-stick baking paper. Sift the flour and baking powder together and set aside.

Cream the butter with the sugar until light and fluffy, then gradually beat in the eggs, adding a little of the flour after each addition. When all the eggs have been added, stir in the remaining flour together with the ground almonds. Sift the drinking chocolate powder into the mixture and stir lightly.

Spoon the mixture into the prepared cake tin and smooth the top. Bake in the preheated oven for 50–55 minutes, or until a skewer, inserted into the centre, comes out clean. Remove from the oven and leave to cool before removing from the tin and discarding the lining paper. Leave until cold.

Sift the icing sugar and cocoa together into a mixing bowl and make a hollow in the centre. Place the butter in the centre. Mix with with sufficient hot water to form a smooth spreadable icing. Coat the top and sides of the cake with icing, swirling it to give a decorative effect. Dust with icing sugar.

---

1 tsp sunflower oil, for oiling
55 g/2 oz self-raising flour
1 tsp baking powder
115 g/4 oz butter or margarine, softened
115 g/4 oz caster sugar
3 eggs, beaten
25 g/1 oz ground almonds
115 g/4 oz drinking chocolate powder
1 tbsp icing sugar, for dusting

ICING
225 g/8 oz icing sugar
1$\frac{1}{2}$ tbsp cocoa powder
2 tbsp butter
3–4 tbsp hot water

Almond & Hazelnut Gâteau

SERVES 8

Preheat the oven to 190°C/375°F/Gas Mark 5. Grease two 18-cm/7-inch sandwich tins and line with greaseproof paper.

Whisk the eggs and caster sugar in a large mixing bowl with an electric whisk for about 10 minutes, or until the mixture is very light and foamy and a trail is left when the whisk is dragged across the surface.

Fold in the ground nuts. Sift the flour and fold in with a metal spoon or palette knife. Divide the mixture between the prepared tins.

Scatter the flaked almonds over the top of one of the cakes. Bake both of the cakes in the preheated oven for 15–20 minutes, or until springy to the touch.

Leave to cool slightly in the tins. Remove the cakes from the tins and transfer to a wire rack to cool completely.

Meanwhile, make the filling. Melt the chocolate, remove from the heat and stir in the butter. Leave the mixture to cool slightly. Whip the cream until just holding its shape, then fold in the melted chocolate until mixed.

Place the cake without the extra almonds on a serving plate and spread the filling over it. Leave the filling to set slightly, then place the almond-topped cake on top and chill for about 1 hour. Dust with icing sugar and serve.

butter, for greasing
4 eggs
115 g/4 oz caster sugar
50 g/1¾ oz ground almonds
50 g/1¾ oz ground hazelnuts
50 g/1¾ oz plain flour
70 g/2½ oz flaked almonds

FILLING
100 g/3½ oz plain chocolate, broken into pieces
1 tbsp butter
300 ml/10 fl oz double cream
icing sugar, for dusting

Mississippi Mud Pie

SERVES 8

To make the pastry, sift the flour and cocoa powder into a mixing bowl. Rub in the butter with the fingertips until the mixture resembles fine breadcrumbs. Stir in the sugar and enough cold water to mix to a soft dough in clingfilm. Wrap the dough and chill in the refrigerator for 15 minutes.

Preheat the oven to 190°C/375°F/Gas Mark 5. Roll out the pastry on a lightly floured work surface and use to line a 23-cm/9-inch loose-based flan tin or ceramic flan dish. Line with greaseproof paper and fill with baking beans. Bake in the preheated oven for 15 minutes. Remove the paper and beans from the pastry case and cook for a further 10 minutes until crisp.

To make the filling, beat the butter and sugar together in a bowl and gradually beat in the eggs with the cocoa powder. Melt the chocolate and beat it into the mixture with the single cream and the chocolate essence.

Reduce the oven temperature to 160°C/325°F/Gas Mark 3. Pour the mixture into the pastry case and bake for 45 minutes, or until the filling has set gently.

Let the mud pie cool completely, then transfer the pie to a serving plate. Cover with the whipped cream. Decorate the pie with chocolate flakes and curls and then chill until ready to serve.

PASTRY

225 g/8 oz plain flour, plus extra
    for dusting
2 tbsp cocoa powder
140 g/5 oz butter
2 tbsp caster sugar
1–2 tbsp cold water

FILLING

175 g/6 oz butter
350 g/12 oz soft dark brown
    sugar
4 eggs, lightly beaten
4 tbsp cocoa powder, sifted
150 g/5½ oz plain chocolate,
    broken into pieces
300 ml/10 fl oz single cream
1 tsp chocolate essence

TO DECORATE

425 ml/15 fl oz double cream,
    whipped
chocolate flakes and curls

Chocolate Crumble Pie

SERVES 8

To make the pastry, sift the flour and baking powder into a large bowl, rub in the butter and stir in the sugar, then add the egg yolk and the water to bring the dough together. Turn the dough out and knead briefly. Wrap the dough in clingfilm and chill in the refrigerator for 30 minutes.

Preheat the oven to 190°C/375°F/Gas Mark 5. Roll out the pastry and use to line a 23-cm/9-inch loose-based flan tin. Prick the base with a fork. Line with greaseproof paper, fill with baking beans and bake in the oven for 15 minutes. Remove the paper and beans. Reduce the oven temperature to 180°C/350°F/Gas Mark 4.

Bring the cream and milk to the boil in a saucepan, remove from the heat and add the chocolate. Stir until melted and smooth. Beat the eggs and add to the chocolate mixture, mix well and pour into the pastry case. Bake for 15 minutes, remove from the oven and leave to rest for 1 hour.

When you are ready to serve the pie, put the crumble topping ingredients into the food processor and pulse to chop. If you do not have a food processor, put the sugar in a large bowl, chop the nuts with a large knife and crush the biscuits, then add to the bowl with the cocoa and mix well. Sprinkle over the pie, then serve it in slices.

PASTRY

175 g/6 oz plain flour

1 tsp baking powder

115 g/4 oz unsalted butter, cut into small pieces

55 g/2 oz caster sugar

1 egg yolk

1–2 tsp cold water

FILLING

150 ml/5 fl oz double cream

150 ml/5 fl oz milk

225 g/8 oz plain chocolate, chopped

2 eggs

CRUMBLE TOPPING

115 g/4 oz soft light brown sugar

85 g/3 oz toasted pecan nuts

115 g/4 oz plain chocolate, chopped

85 g/3 oz amaretti biscuits

1 tsp cocoa powder

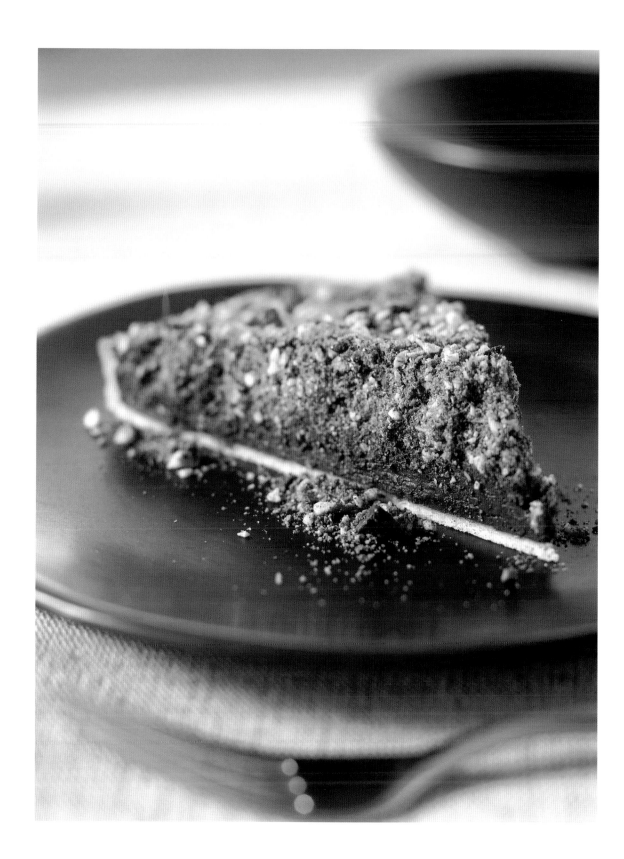

Blackberry Chocolate Flan

SERVES 6

To make the pastry, sift the flour, cocoa powder, icing sugar and salt into a mixing bowl and make a well in the centre. Put the butter and egg yolk in the well and gradually mix in the dry ingredients, using a pastry blender or 2 forks. Knead lightly and form into a ball. Wrap the dough and chill in the refrigerator for 1 hour.

Preheat the oven to 180°C/350°F/Gas Mark 4. Roll out the pastry on a lightly floured work surface. Use it to line a 30 x 10-cm/12 x 4-inch rectangular flan tin and prick the pastry case with a fork. Line the base with greaseproof paper and fill with baking beans. Bake in the preheated oven for 15 minutes. Take out of the oven and remove the paper and beans. Set aside to cool.

To make the filling, put the cream and jam in a saucepan and bring to the boil over a low heat. Remove the saucepan from the heat and stir in the chocolate and then the butter until melted and smooth. Pour the mixture into the pastry case and set aside to cool.

To make the sauce, put the blackberries, lemon juice and caster sugar in a food processor and process until smooth. Strain through a nylon sieve into a bowl and stir in the cassis. Set aside.

Remove the flan from the tin and place on a serving plate. Arrange the remaining blackberries on top and brush with a little of the blackberry and liqueur sauce. Serve the flan with the remaining sauce on the side.

PASTRY

140 g/5 oz plain flour, plus extra
 for dusting
25 g/1 oz cocoa powder
55 g/2 oz icing sugar
pinch of salt
85 g/3 oz butter, cut into small
 pieces
1/2 egg yolk

FILLING

300 ml/10 fl oz double cream
175 g/6 oz blackberry jam
225 g/8 oz plain chocolate,
 broken into pieces
25 g/1 oz unsalted butter, cut
 into small pieces

SAUCE

675 g/1 lb 8 oz blackberries, plus
 extra to decorate
1 tbsp lemon juice
2 tbsp caster sugar
2 tbsp crème de cassis

Toffee Chocolate Puff Tarts

MAKES 12

Line the bases of a 12-hole non-stick muffin tin with discs of greaseproof paper.

Cut out twelve 5 cm/2-inch circles from the edge of the pastry and cut the remainder into 12 strips. Roll the strips to half their thickness and line the sides of each hole with 1 strip. Put a disc of pastry in each base, and press well together to seal and make a tart case. Prick the bases and chill in the refrigerator for 30 minutes.

Preheat the oven to 200°C/400°F/Gas Mark 6. While the pastry is chilling, melt the chocolate in a heatproof bowl set over a saucepan of gently simmering water. Remove the bowl from the heat, cool slightly, then stir in the cream. Beat the sugar and egg yolks together and mix well with the melted chocolate.

Remove the muffin tin from the refrigerator and put a teaspoonful of the toffee sauce into each tart case. Divide the chocolate mixture between the tarts and bake in the preheated oven for 20–25 minutes, turning the tray around halfway through cooking, until just set. Remove from the oven and cool the tarts in the tin. Remove the tarts from the tin carefully, leaving behind the greaseproof paper. Dust with cocoa powder and serve with whipped cream.

375 g/13 oz ready-rolled puff pastry
140 g/5 oz plain chocolate, broken into pieces
300 ml/10 fl oz double cream
50 g/1¾ oz caster sugar
4 egg yolks
4 tbsp ready-made toffee sauce
cocoa powder, for dusting
whipped cream, to serve

Black Forest Roulade

SERVES 8–10

Preheat the oven to 190°C/375°F/Gas Mark 5. Grease and line a Swiss roll tin with 1 whole sheet of greaseproof paper. Break the chocolate into small pieces and place in a heatproof bowl set over a saucepan of gently simmering water. Add the kirsch and heat gently, stirring until the mixture is smooth. Remove from the pan and set aside.

Place the eggs and sugar in a large heatproof bowl and set over the saucepan of gently simmering water. Alternatively, place in the heatproof bowl of a free-standing mixer and use a balloon whisk. Whisk the eggs and sugar until very thick and creamy and the whisk leaves a trail when dragged across the surface. Remove the bowl from the heat and whisk in the cooled chocolate.

Spoon into the prepared Swiss roll tin, then tap the tin lightly on the work surface to smooth the top. Bake in the preheated oven for 20 minutes, or until the top feels firm to the touch. Remove from the oven and immediately invert on to a whole sheet of greaseproof paper that has been sprinkled with the icing sugar. Lift off the tin and lining paper, then roll up, encasing the greaseproof paper in the roulade. Leave until cold.

For the filling, whip the cream until soft peaks form, then stir in the kirsch reserving 1–2 tablespoons. Unroll the roulade and spread over the cream to within 1/4 inch/5 mm of the edges. Scatter the cherries over the cream. Carefully roll up the roulade again and place on a serving platter.

1 tsp sunflower oil, for oiling
175 g/6 oz plain chocolate
2–3 tbsp kirsch or brandy
5 eggs
225 g/8 oz caster sugar
2 tbsp icing sugar, sifted

FILLING
350 ml/12 fl oz double cream
2–3 tbsp kirsch or brandy
350 g/12 oz fresh black cherries, stoned, or 400 g/14 oz canned morello cherries, drained and stoned

Cappuccino Soufflé Puddings

MAKES 6

Preheat the oven to 190°C/375°F/Gas Mark 5. Grease the sides of six 175-ml/ 6-fl oz ramekin dishes with butter and coat with the extra caster sugar. Place on a baking tray. Place the cream in a saucepan and warm gently. Stir in the coffee until dissolved, then add the Kahlúa. Divide the mixture among the prepared ramekin dishes.

In a clean, greasefree bowl, whisk the egg whites until soft peaks form, then gradually whisk in the caster sugar until stiff and glossy but not dry. Put the chocolate in a heatproof bowl set over a saucepan of gently simmering water until melted. Add the egg yolks to the melted chocolate, then stir in a little of the whisked egg whites.

Gradually fold in the egg whites. Divide the mixture between the ramekins. Cook in the preheated oven for 15 minutes until just set. Dust with cocoa powder and serve immediately.

butter, for greasing

25 g/1 oz caster sugar, plus extra for coating

6 tbsp whipping cream

2 tsp instant espresso coffee granules

2 tbsp Kahlúa

3 large eggs, separated, plus 1 extra white

150 g/5½ oz plain chocolate, broken into pieces

cocoa powder, for dusting

Baked to Perfection

Double Chocolate Muffins

MAKES 12

Preheat the oven to 200°C/400°F/Gas Mark 6. Line a 12-cup muffin tin with muffin paper cases. Sift the flour, cocoa, baking powder and cinnamon into a large mixing bowl. Stir in the sugar and 125 g/4½ oz of the white chocolate.

Place the eggs and oil in a separate bowl and whisk until frothy, then gradually whisk in the milk. Stir into the dry ingredients until just blended. Spoon the mixture into the paper cases, filling each three-quarters full. Bake in the preheated oven for 20 minutes, or until well risen and springy to the touch. Leave to cool for 2 minutes, then remove the muffins and transfer to a wire rack to cool completely.

Melt the remaining white chocolate in a heatproof bowl set over a saucepan of gently simmering water until melted and spread over the top of the muffins. Leave to set, then dust the tops with a little cocoa and serve.

200 g/7 oz plain flour
25 g/1 oz cocoa powder, plus extra for dusting
1 tbsp baking powder
1 tsp ground cinnamon
115 g/4 oz caster sugar
185 g/6½ oz white chocolate, broken into pieces
2 eggs
100 ml/3½ fl oz sunflower oil
225 ml/8 fl oz milk

Spiced Chocolate Muffins

MAKES 12

Line a 12-cup muffin tin with muffin paper cases.

Place the butter, caster sugar and brown sugar in a bowl and beat well. Beat in the eggs, soured cream and milk until thoroughly mixed. Sift the flour, bicarbonate of soda, cocoa and allspice into a separate bowl and stir into the mixture. Add the chocolate chips and mix well. Divide the mixture evenly between the paper cases. Bake in a preheated oven, 190°C/375°F/Gas Mark 5, for 25–30 minutes.

Remove from the oven and cool for 10 minutes, then transfer to a wire rack to cool completely. Store in an airtight container until required.

100 g/3$\frac{1}{2}$ oz butter, softened

150 g/5$\frac{1}{2}$ oz caster sugar

115 g/4 oz brown sugar

2 large eggs

150 ml/5 fl oz soured cream

5 tbsp milk

250 g/9 oz plain flour

1 tsp bicarbonate of soda

2 tbsp cocoa powder

1 tsp allspice

200 g/7 oz plain chocolate chips

Triple Chocolate Muffins

MAKES 12

Preheat the oven to 200°C/400°F/Gas Mark 6. Line a 12-cup muffin tin with muffin paper cases. Sift the flour, cocoa, baking powder and bicarbonate of soda into a large bowl, then stir in the plain and white chocolate chips.

Place the eggs, soured cream, sugar and butter in a separate mixing bowl and mix well. Add the wet ingredients to the dry ingredients and stir gently until just combined.

Using 2 spoons, divide the mixture between the paper cases and bake in the preheated oven for 20 minutes, or until well risen and firm to the touch. Serve warm or cold.

250 g/9 oz plain flour
25 g/1 oz cocoa powder
2 tsp baking powder
$\frac{1}{2}$ tsp bicarbonate of soda
100 g/3$\frac{1}{2}$ oz plain chocolate chips
100 g/3$\frac{1}{2}$ oz white chocolate chips
2 eggs, beaten
300 ml/10 fl oz soured cream
85 g/3 oz light muscovado sugar
85 g/3 oz butter, melted

Marshmallow Muffins

MAKES 12

Preheat the oven to 190°C/375°F/Gas Mark 5. Place 12 muffin paper cases in a muffin tin. Melt the butter.

Sift the flour, cocoa and baking powder together into a large bowl. Stir in the sugar.

Whisk the egg, milk and melted butter together, then gently stir into the flour mixture to form a stiff batter. Gently stir in the chocolate chips and marshmallows. Spoon the mixture into the muffin cases.

Bake the muffins in the preheated oven for 20–25 minutes, until well risen. Leave to cool in the tin for 5 minutes, then transfer to a wire rack and leave to cool completely.

70 g/2$\frac{1}{2}$ oz butter
280 g/10 oz plain flour
6 tbsp cocoa powder
3 tsp baking powder
85 g/3 oz caster sugar
1 egg, beaten
300 ml/10 fl oz milk
100 g/3$\frac{1}{2}$ oz milk chocolate chips
55 g/2 oz white mini marshmallows

Chocolate Brownies

MAKES 15

Preheat the oven to 180°C/350°F/Gas Mark 4. Grease and line a 28 x 18-cm/11 x 7-inch rectangular cake tin.

Put the butter and dark chocolate pieces into a heatproof bowl and set over a saucepan of simmering water until melted. Remove from the heat. Sift the flour into a large bowl, add the sugar and mix well. Stir the eggs into the chocolate mixture, then beat into the flour mixture. Add the nuts, sultanas and chocolate chips and mix well. Spoon evenly into the cake tin and level the surface.

Bake in the preheated oven for 30 minutes, or until firm. To check whether the cake is cooked through, insert a skewer into the centre – it should come out clean. If not, return the cake to the oven for a few more minutes. Remove from the oven and leave to cool for 15 minutes. Turn out on to a wire rack to cool completely. To decorate, drizzle the melted white chocolate in fine lines over the cake, then cut into squares. Leave to set before serving.

225 g/8 oz butter, diced,
   plus extra for greasing
150 g/5^1/$_2$ oz dark chocolate,
   chopped
225 g/8 oz self-raising flour
125 g/4^1/$_2$ oz dark muscovado
   sugar
4 eggs, beaten
60 g/2^1/$_4$ oz blanched
   hazelnuts, chopped
60 g/2^1/$_4$ oz sultanas
100 g/3^1/$_2$ oz dark
   chocolate chips
115 g/4 oz white chocolate,
   melted, to decorate

Chocolate Fudge Brownies

MAKES 16

Preheat the oven to 180°C/350°F/Gas Mark 4. Lightly grease and line a
20-cm/8-inch square, shallow cake pan.

Beat together the cheese, vanilla essence and 5 teaspoons of caster sugar until
smooth, then set aside.

Beat the eggs and remaining caster sugar together until light and fluffy. Place
the butter and cocoa powder in a small pan and heat gently, stirring until the
butter melts and the mixture combines, then stir it into the egg mixture. Fold in
the flour and nuts.

Pour half of the cake batter into the prepared pan and smooth the top.
Carefully spread the cheese mixture over it, then cover it with the remaining
cake batter. Bake in the preheated oven for 40–45 minutes. Leave to cool in
the pan.

To make the icing, melt the butter in the milk. Stir in the icing sugar and cocoa
powder. Spread the icing over the brownies and decorate with pecan nuts, if
using. Let the icing set, then cut into rectangles or squares to serve.

85 g/3 oz butter,
  plus extra for greasing
200 g/7 oz low-fat soft cheese
1/2 tsp vanilla essence
225 g/8 oz caster sugar
2 eggs
3 tbsp cocoa powder
100 g/3 1/2 oz self-raising flour,
  sifted
50 g/1 3/4 oz pecan nuts, chopped

FUDGE ICING
4 tbsp butter
1 tbsp milk
75 g/2 3/4 oz icing sugar
2 tbsp cocoa powder
pecan nuts, to decorate
  (optional)

Black Russian Brownies

MAKES 8–10

Preheat the oven to 180°C/350°F/Gas Mark 4. Grease and base-line a 30 x 20-cm/12 x 8-inch shallow cake tin with non-stick baking paper.

Melt the chocolate and the butter with the pepper in a small saucepan over a low heat. Remove from the heat and cool slightly.

Beat together the eggs, sugar and vanilla essence in a large bowl and stir in the chocolate mixture, Kahlùa and vodka.

Sift the flour and baking powder together and stir evenly into the chocolate mixture. Stir in the walnuts. Pour into the prepared tin and bake in the preheated oven for 20–25 minutes, until just firm to the touch.

Cool for a few minutes then cut into rectangles or squares and lift carefully from the tin on to serving plates.

For the topping, stir the Kahlùa into the crème fraîche and spoon a generous dollop on each brownie. Dust with a little cocoa powder and serve immediately.

115 g/4 oz butter, plus extra for greasing
115 g/4 oz plain chocolate, broken into pieces
1/2 tsp coarsely ground black peppercorns
4 eggs, beaten
250 g/9 oz caster sugar
1 tsp vanilla essence
3 tbsp Kahlùa liqueur
2 tbsp vodka
150 g/5 1/2 oz plain flour
1/4 tsp baking powder
55 g/2 oz walnuts, chopped

KAHLUA TOPPING
2 tbsp Kahlùa
200 g/7 oz crème fraîche
cocoa powder, for dusting

Chocolate Butterfly Cakes

MAKES 12

Preheat the oven to 180°C/350°F/Gas Mark 4. Put 12 paper baking cases in a bun tray, or put 12 double-layer paper cases on a baking tray.

Put the margarine, sugar, flour, eggs and cocoa powder in a large bowl and, using an electric hand whisk, beat together until just smooth. Beat in the melted chocolate. Spoon the mixture into the paper cases, filling them three-quarters full.

Bake the cupcakes in the preheated oven for 15 minutes, or until springy to the touch. Transfer to a wire rack and leave to cool.

To make the filling, put the butter in a bowl and beat until fluffy. Sift in the icing sugar and beat together until smooth. Add the melted chocolate and beat together until well mixed.

When the cupcakes are cold, use a serrated knife to cut a circle from the top of each cake and then cut each circle in half. Spread or pipe a little of the butter cream into the centre of each cupcake and press 2 semi-circular halves into it at an angle to resemble butterfly wings. Dust with sifted icing sugar before serving.

125 g/4½ oz soft tub margarine
125 g/4½ oz caster sugar
150 g/5½ oz self-raising flour
2 large eggs
2 tbsp cocoa powder
25 g/1 oz plain chocolate, melted
icing sugar, sifted, for dusting

FILLING
85 g/3 oz butter, softened
175 g/6 oz icing sugar
25 g/1 oz plain chocolate, melted

Dark & White Fudge Cupcakes

MAKES 20

Preheat the oven to 180°C/350°F/Gas Mark 4. Put 20 paper baking cases in 2 bun trays, or put 20 double-layer paper cases on 2 baking trays.

Put the water, butter, sugar and syrup in a saucepan. Heat gently, stirring, until the sugar has dissolved, then bring to the boil. Reduce the heat and cook gently for 5 minutes. Remove from the heat and leave to cool.

Meanwhile, put the milk and vanilla essence in a bowl. Add the bicarbonate of soda and stir to dissolve. Sift the flour and cocoa powder into a separate bowl and add the syrup mixture. Stir in the milk and beat until smooth. Spoon the mixture into the paper cases until they are two-thirds full.

Bake the cupcakes in the preheated oven for 20 minutes, or until well risen and firm to the touch. Transfer to a wire rack and leave to cool.

To make the icing, break the plain chocolate into a small heatproof bowl, add half the water and half the butter, and set the bowl over a saucepan of gently simmering water until melted. Stir until smooth and leave to stand over the water. Repeat with the white chocolate and remaining water and butter. Sift half the icing sugar into each bowl and beat until smooth and thick. Top the cupcakes with the icing then leave to set. Serve decorated with chocolate shavings.

200 ml/7 fl oz water
85 g/3 oz butter
85 g/3 oz caster sugar
1 tbsp golden syrup
3 tbsp milk
1 tsp vanilla essence
1 tsp bicarbonate of soda
225 g/8 oz plain flour
2 tbsp cocoa powder

ICING
50 g/1¾ oz plain chocolate
4 tbsp water
50 g/1¾ oz butter
50 g/1¾ oz white chocolate
350 g/12 oz icing sugar

TO DECORATE
100 g/3½ oz plain chocolate
  shavings
100 g/3½ oz white chocolate
  shavings

Chocolate Cupcakes with Cream Cheese Icing

MAKES 18

Preheat the oven to 200°C/400°F/Gas Mark 6. Put 18 paper baking cases in 2 bun trays, or put 18 double-layer paper cases on a baking tray.

Put the butter and sugar in a bowl and beat together until light and fluffy. Gradually add the eggs, beating well after each addition. Add the milk, then fold in the chocolate chips. Sift in the flour and cocoa powder together, then fold into the mixture. Spoon the mixture into the paper cases and smooth the tops.

Bake the cupcakes in the preheated oven for 20 minutes, or until well risen and springy to the touch. Transfer to a wire rack and leave to cool.

To make the icing, break the chocolate into a small heatproof bowl and set the bowl over a saucepan of gently simmering water until melted. Leave to cool slightly. Put the cream cheese in a bowl and beat until softened, then beat in the slightly cooled chocolate.

Spread a little of the icing over the top of each cupcake, then leave to chill in the refrigerator for 1 hour before serving. Serve decorated with the chocolate curls.

85 g/3 oz butter, softened, or
   soft tub margarine
100 g/3¹/₂ oz caster sugar
2 eggs, lightly beaten
2 tbsp milk
55 g/2 oz plain chocolate chips
225 g/8 oz self-raising flour
25 g/1 oz cocoa powder

ICING
225 g/8 oz white chocolate
150 g/5¹/₂ oz low-fat cream
   cheese
chocolate curls, to decorate

Crumbly Cookies & Heavenly Bites

Chocolate Chip Cookies

MAKES 20

Preheat the oven to 180°C/350°F/Gas Mark 4. Grease 2 large baking sheets. Place the butter and sugar in a bowl and beat together with a wooden spoon until light and fluffy.

Beat in the egg, then add the oats, milk and vanilla essence. Beat together until well blended. Sift the flour, cocoa and baking powder into the mixture and stir. Stir in the chocolate pieces.

Place dessertspoonfuls of the mixture on the prepared baking sheets and flatten slightly with a fork. Bake in the preheated oven for 15 minutes, or until slightly risen and firm. Remove from the oven, cool on the baking sheets for 2 minutes, then transfer to wire racks to cool completely.

115 g/4 oz butter, softened, plus extra for greasing
115 g/4 oz light muscovado sugar
1 egg
100 g/3$\frac{1}{2}$ oz porridge oats
1 tbsp milk
1 tsp vanilla essence
125 g/4$\frac{1}{2}$ oz plain flour
1 tbsp cocoa powder
$\frac{1}{2}$ tsp baking powder
175 g/6 oz plain chocolate, broken into pieces
175 g/6 oz milk chocolate, broken into pieces

Double Chocolate Chip Cookies

MAKES 24

Preheat the oven to 180°C/350°F/Gas Mark 4. Grease 2 baking sheets with butter. Place the butter, sugar and vanilla essence in a large bowl and beat together. Gradually beat in the egg until the mixture is light and fluffy.

Sift the flour, salt and bicarbonate of soda over the mixture and fold in. Fold in the chocolate chips.

Drop heaped teaspoonfuls of the mixture on to the prepared baking sheets, allowing room for the cookies to spread during cooking. Bake in the preheated oven for 10–12 minutes, or until crisp outside but still soft inside. Leave to cool on the baking sheets for 2 minutes, then transfer to wire racks to cool completely.

200 g/7 oz butter, softened, plus
   extra for greasing
200 g/7 oz caster sugar
1/2 tsp vanilla essence
1 large egg
225 g/8 oz plain flour
pinch of salt
1 tsp bicarbonate of soda
115 g/4 oz white chocolate chips
115 g/4 oz plain chocolate chips

Chocolate Orange Cookies

MAKES 30

Preheat the oven to 180°C/350°F/Gas Mark 4. Line 2 baking sheets with sheets of greaseproof paper.

Beat together the butter and sugar until the mixture is light and fluffy. Beat in the egg and milk until well combined. Sift the flour and cocoa into the bowl and gradually mix together to form a soft dough. Use your fingers to incorporate the last of the flour and bring the dough together.

Roll out the dough on a lightly floured work surface until 5 mm/¹/₄ inch thick. Cut out circles using a 5-cm/2-inch fluted round biscuit cutter.

Place the circles on the prepared baking sheets and bake in the preheated oven for 10–12 minutes, or until golden.

Let the biscuits cool on the baking sheet for a few minutes before transferring them to a wire rack to cool completely and become crisp.

To make the icing, put the icing sugar in a bowl and stir in enough orange juice to form a thin icing that will coat the back of the spoon. Put a spoonful of icing in the centre of each biscuit and leave to set. Place the plain chocolate in a heatproof bowl set over a saucepan of gently simmering water and stir until melted. Drizzle thin lines of melted chocolate over the biscuits and leave to set before serving.

90 g/3¹/₄ oz butter, softened
60 g/2¹/₄ oz caster sugar
1 egg
1 tbsp milk
280 g/10 oz plain flour, plus extra
  for dusting
2 tbsp cocoa powder

ICING
175 g/6 oz icing sugar, sifted
3 tbsp orange juice
a little plain chocolate, broken
  into pieces

White Chocolate Cookies

MAKES 24

Preheat the oven to 190°C/375°F/Gas Mark 5. Grease several baking sheets lightly with a little butter.

In a large mixing bowl, cream together the butter and sugar until light and fluffy.

Gradually add the beaten egg to the creamed mixture, beating well after each addition.

Sift the flour and salt into the creamed mixture and blend well.

Stir in the white chocolate chunks and the chopped Brazil nuts.

Place heaped teaspoonfuls of the mixture on the prepared baking sheets. Put no more than 6 on each sheet because the cookies will spread during cooking.

Bake in the oven for 10–12 minutes, or until just golden brown.

Transfer the cookies to wire racks and leave until completely cold.

115 g/4 oz butter, softened, plus
    extra for greasing
115 g/4 oz soft brown sugar
1 egg, beaten
250 g/9 oz self-raising flour
pinch of salt
125 g/4$\frac{1}{2}$ oz white chocolate,
    chopped
50 g/1$\frac{3}{4}$ oz chopped Brazil nuts

Chocolate & Coffee Wholemeal Cookies

MAKES 24

Preheat the oven to 190°C/375°F/Gas Mark 5. Grease 2 large baking sheets. Cream the butter and sugar together in a bowl. Add the egg and beat well, using a hand whisk if preferred.

In a separate bowl, sift together the plain flour, bicarbonate of soda and salt, then add in the wholemeal flour and bran. Mix in the egg mixture, then stir in the chocolate chips, oats, coffee and hazelnuts. Mix well, with an electric whisk if preferred.

Put 24 rounded tablespoonfuls of the mixture on to the prepared baking sheets, allowing room for the biscuits to spread during cooking. Alternatively, with lightly floured hands, break off pieces of the mixture and roll into balls (about 25 g/1 oz each), place on the baking sheets and flatten them with the back of a teaspoon.

Transfer the baking sheets to the preheated oven and bake for 16–18 minutes, or until the biscuits are golden brown.

Remove from the oven, transfer the biscuits to a wire rack and leave to cool before serving.

175 g/6 oz butter or margarine, plus extra for greasing
200 g/7 oz soft brown sugar
1 egg
70 g/2$\frac{1}{2}$ oz plain flour
1 tsp bicarbonate of soda
pinch of salt
70 g/2$\frac{1}{2}$ oz wholemeal flour
1 tbsp bran
225 g/8 oz plain chocolate chips
185 g/6$\frac{1}{2}$ oz rolled oats
1 tbsp strong coffee
100 g/3$\frac{1}{2}$ oz hazelnuts, toasted and roughly chopped

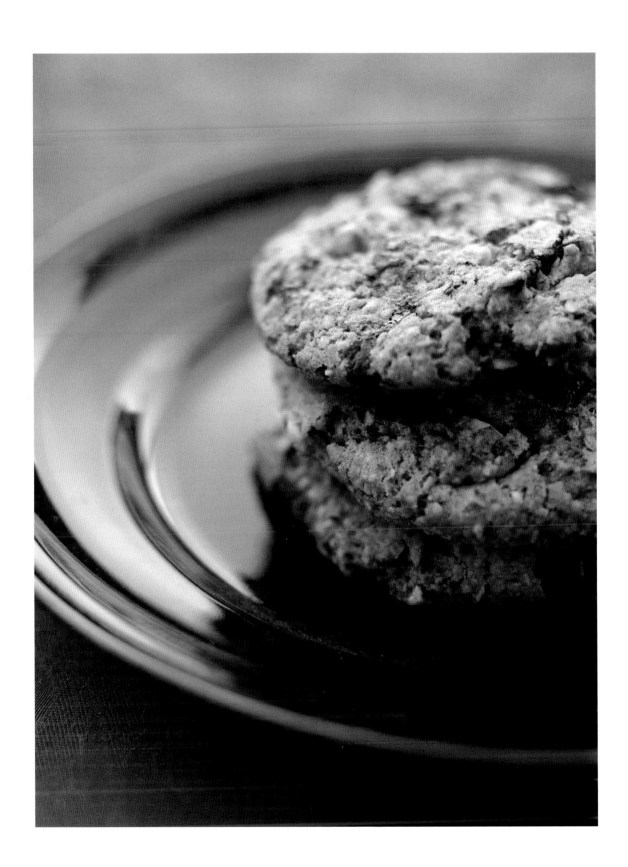

Chocolate Peanut Butter Slices

MAKES 26

Preheat the oven to 180°C/350°F/Gas Mark 4. Finely chop the chocolate. Sift the flour and baking powder into a large bowl.

Add the butter to the flour and rub in until the mixture resembles breadcrumbs. Stir in the sugar, oats and chopped nuts.

Put a quarter of the mixture into a bowl and stir in the chopped chocolate. Set aside.

Stir the egg into the remaining mixture, then press into the bottom of a 30 x 20-cm/12 x 8-inch roasting tin.

Bake the base in the preheated oven for 15 minutes. Meanwhile, mix the condensed milk and peanut butter together. Pour the mixture over the base and spread evenly, then sprinkle the reserved chocolate mixture on top and press down lightly.

Return to the oven and bake for an additional 20 minutes, until golden brown. Leave to cool in the tin, then cut into slices.

300 g/10$\frac{1}{2}$ oz milk chocolate
350 g/12 oz plain flour
1 tsp baking powder
225 g/8 oz butter
350 g/12 oz soft brown sugar
175 g/6 oz rolled oats
70 g/2$\frac{1}{2}$ oz chopped mixed nuts
1 egg, beaten
400 ml/14 fl oz condensed milk
70 g/2$\frac{1}{2}$ oz crunchy peanut
   butter

Chocolate Wheatmeals

MAKES 20

Preheat the oven to 180°C/350°F/Gas Mark 4. Lightly grease a baking sheet. Beat the butter and sugar until fluffy. Add the egg and beat well. Stir in the wheatgerm and flours. Bring the mixture together with your hands.

Roll rounded teaspoonfuls of the mixture into balls and place on the prepared baking sheet, allowing room for the biscuits to spread during cooking.

Flatten the biscuits slightly with the tines of a fork. Bake in the preheated oven for 15–20 minutes, until golden. Leave to cool on the baking sheet for a few minutes before transferring to a wire rack to cool completely.

Put the chocolate in a heatproof bowl set over a saucepan of gently simmering water until melted. Dip each biscuit in the chocolate to cover the flat side and a little way around the edges. Let the excess drip back into the bowl.

Place the biscuits on a sheet of greaseproof paper in a cool place and leave the chocolate to set before serving.

75 g/2¾ oz butter, plus extra for greasing
125 g/4½ oz Demerara sugar
1 egg
1 tbsp wheatgerm
150 g/5½ oz wholewheat self-raising flour
70 g/2½ oz self-raising flour, sifted
125 g/4½ oz chocolate, broken into pieces

Chocolate Caramel Squares

MAKES 16

Preheat the oven to 180°C/350°F/Gas Mark 4. Beat together the margarine and brown sugar in a bowl until light and fluffy. Beat in the flour and the rolled oats. Use your fingertips to bring the mixture together, if necessary.

Press the mixture into the base of a greased 20-cm/8-inch square, shallow cake tin.

Bake the mixture in the preheated oven for 25 minutes, or until just golden and firm. Cool in the tin.

Place the ingredients for the caramel filling in a saucepan and heat gently, stirring until the sugar has dissolved. Bring slowly to the boil over a very low heat, then boil very gently for 3–4 minutes, stirring constantly, until thickened.

Pour the caramel filling over the oat layer in the tin and leave to set.

Melt the plain chocolate and spread it over the caramel. If using the white chocolate, place in a heatproof bowl set over a saucepan of gently simmering water until melted. Pipe lines of white chocolate over the plain chocolate. Using a cocktail stick, feather the white chocolate into the plain chocolate. Leave to set, then cut into squares to serve.

75 g/2¾ oz margarine, plus
   extra for greasing
60 g/2¼ oz soft brown sugar
140 g/5 oz plain flour
40 g/1½ oz rolled oats

CARAMEL FILLING
2 tbsp butter
2 tbsp soft brown sugar
225 ml/8 fl oz condensed milk

TOPPING
100 g/3½ oz plain chocolate
25 g/1 oz white chocolate
   (optional)

Chocolate Chip Flapjacks

MAKES 12

Preheat the oven to 180°C/350°F/Gas Mark 4. Lightly grease a 20-cm/8-inch square, shallow cake tin.

Place the butter, caster sugar and golden syrup in a saucepan and cook over a low heat, stirring constantly, until the butter and sugar melt and the mixture is well combined.

Remove the saucepan from the heat and stir in the rolled oats until they are well coated. Add the chocolate chips and the sultanas and mix well to combine everything.

Turn into the prepared tin and press down well.

Bake in the preheated oven for 30 minutes. Cool slightly, then mark into squares. When almost cold, cut into squares and transfer to a wire rack to cool completely.

115 g/4 oz butter, plus extra for greasing
60 g/2¼ oz caster sugar
1 tbsp golden syrup
350 g/12 oz rolled oats
85 g/3 oz plain chocolate chips
85 g/3 oz sultanas

Cool Chocolate

Chocolate Chip Ice Cream with Hot Chocolate Fudge Sauce

SERVES 4–6

Pour the milk into a heavy-based saucepan, add the vanilla pod and bring almost to the boil. Remove from the heat and leave to infuse for 30 minutes. Meanwhile, chop the chocolate into small pieces and set aside.

Put the sugar and egg yolks in a large bowl and whisk together until pale and the mixture leaves a trail when the whisk is lifted. Remove the vanilla pod from the milk, then slowly add the milk to the sugar mixture, stirring all the time with a wooden spoon. Strain the mixture into the rinsed-out saucepan or a double boiler and cook over a low heat for 10–15 minutes, stirring all the time, until the mixture thickens enough to coat the back of the spoon. Do not boil or it will curdle.

Remove the custard from the heat and leave to cool for at least 1 hour, stirring from time to time to prevent a skin from forming. Meanwhile, whip the cream until it holds its shape. Keep in the refrigerator until ready to use.

If using an ice cream machine, fold the cold custard into the whipped cream, then churn the mixture in the machine following the manufacturer's instructions. Just before the ice cream freezes, add the chocolate pieces. Alternatively, freeze the custard in a freezerproof container, uncovered, for 1–2 hours, or until it begins to set around the edges. Turn the custard into a bowl and stir with a fork or beat in a food processor until smooth. Fold in the whipped cream and chocolate pieces. Return to the freezer and freeze for a further 2–3 hours, or until firm or required. Cover the container with a lid for storing.

Make the chocolate sauce just before you serve the ice cream. Put the chocolate, butter and milk in a heatproof bowl set over a saucepan of simmering water and heat gently, stirring occasionally, until the chocolate has melted and the sauce is smooth. Transfer the mixture to a heavy-based saucepan and stir in the sugar and syrup. Heat gently until the sugar has dissolved, then bring to the boil and boil, without stirring, for 5 minutes.

Serve the hot sauce poured over the ice cream.

300 ml/10 fl oz full-fat milk
1 vanilla pod
115 g/4 oz milk chocolate
85 g/3 oz caster sugar
3 egg yolks
300 ml/10 fl oz whipping cream

CHOCOLATE FUDGE SAUCE
50 g/1¾ oz milk chocolate, broken into pieces
25 g/1 oz butter
4 tbsp full-fat milk
225 g/8 oz soft light brown sugar
2 tbsp golden syrup

Chocolate Ice Cream Roll

SERVES 8

Line a 38 x 25-cm/15 x 10-inch Swiss roll tin with greaseproof paper. Grease the bottom and dust with flour. Put the eggs and caster sugar in a heatproof bowl set over a saucepan of simmering water. Whisk over a low heat for 5–10 minutes until the mixture is pale and fluffy. Remove from the heat and continue whisking for 10 minutes until the mixture is cool and the whisk leaves a ribbon trail when lifted. Sift the flour and cocoa powder over the surface and fold them in, gently.

Preheat the oven to 190°C/375°F/Gas Mark 5. Pour the mixture into the prepared tin and spread out evenly with a spatula. Bake in the preheated oven for 15 minutes, until firm to the touch and starting to shrink from the sides of the tin.

Spread out a clean cloth and cover with a sheet of greaseproof paper. Lightly dust with icing sugar. Turn out the cake on to the greaseproof paper and carefully peel off the lining paper. Trim off any crusty edges. Starting from a short side, pick up the cake and the greaseproof paper and roll them up together. Wrap the cloth around the rolled cake and place on a wire rack to cool.

Remove the ice cream from the freezer and put it in the refrigerator for 15–20 minutes to soften slightly. Remove the cloth and unroll the cake. Remove the greaseproof paper and spread the ice cream evenly over the cake, then roll it up again, this time without the greaseproof paper. Wrap the cake in foil and place in the freezer.

Remove the cake from the freezer about 20 minutes before serving. Unwrap, place on a serving plate and dust with icing sugar. Arrange the chocolate caraque over the top. Place the cake in the refrigerator 15 minutes before serving to soften slightly.

butter, for greasing
115 g/4 oz plain flour, plus extra
   for dusting
4 eggs
115 g/4 oz caster sugar
3 tbsp cocoa powder
icing sugar, for dusting
600 g/1 lb 5 oz chocolate
   ice cream
marbled chocolate caraque,
   to decorate

Chocolate Ice Cream Bombe

SERVES 4

Put a 1.4-litre/2^{1}/$_{2}$-pint bombe mould into the freezer. Place the eggs, egg yolks and sugar in a heatproof bowl and beat together until well blended. Put the single cream and chocolate in a saucepan and heat gently until the chocolate has melted, then continue to heat, stirring until almost boiling. Pour on to the egg mixture, stirring vigorously, then place the bowl over a saucepan of simmering water, making sure that the bottom of the bowl does not touch the water. Cook, stirring, until the mixture coats the back of the spoon. Strain into another bowl and leave to cool. Place the double cream in a bowl and whisk until slightly thickened, then fold into the cooled chocolate mixture.

Freeze in an ice-cream maker, following the manufacturer's directions. Alternatively, pour the mixture into a freezerproof container, cover and freeze for 2 hours until just frozen. Spoon into a bowl and beat with a fork to break down the ice crystals. Return to the freezer until almost solid. Line the bombe mould with the chocolate ice cream and return to the freezer.

To make the white chocolate ice cream, put the chocolate and half the milk in a saucepan and heat gently until the chocolate has just melted. Remove from the heat and stir. Put the sugar and remaining milk in another saucepan and heat gently until the sugar has melted. Set aside to cool, then stir into the cooled chocolate mixture. Place the cream in a bowl and whisk until slightly thickened, then fold into the chocolate mixture. Spoon into the centre of the bombe, cover and freeze for about 4 hours, until firm. To serve, dip the mould briefly into warm water, then turn out on to a serving plate. Decorate with chocolate shapes.

PLAIN CHOCOLATE ICE CREAM
2 eggs
2 egg yolks
115 g/4 oz caster sugar
300 ml/10 fl oz single cream
225 g/8 oz plain chocolate,
    chopped
300 ml/10 fl oz double cream

WHITE CHOCOLATE ICE CREAM
140 g/5 oz white chocolate,
    broken into pieces
150 ml/5 fl oz milk
55 g/2 oz golden caster sugar
300 ml/10 fl oz double cream
chocolate shapes, to decorate

Chocolate Ice Cream Bites

SERVES 6

Line a baking tray with clingfilm.

Using a melon baller, scoop out balls of ice cream and place them on the prepared baking tray. Alternatively, cut the ice cream into bite-sized cubes. Stick a cocktail stick in each piece and return to the freezer until very hard.

Place the chocolate and the butter in a heatproof bowl set over a saucepan of gently simmering water until melted. Quickly dip the frozen ice cream balls or cubes into the warm chocolate and return to the freezer. Keep them there until ready to serve.

600 g/1 lb 5 oz good-quality ice cream
200 g/7 oz dark chocolate
2 tbsp unsalted butter

White Chocolate Terrine

SERVES 8

Line a 450-g/1-lb loaf tin with foil or clingfilm pressing out as many creases as you can.

Place the granulated sugar and water in a heavy-based saucepan and heat gently, stirring until the sugar has dissolved. Bring to the boil and boil for 1–2 minutes until syrupy, then remove from the heat.

Break the white chocolate into small pieces and stir it into the hot syrup, continuing to stir until the chocolate has melted and combined with the syrup. Let the mixture cool slightly.

Beat the egg yolks into the chocolate mixture. Leave to cool completely.

Lightly whip the cream until it is just holding its shape, and fold it into the chocolate mixture.

Whisk the egg whites in a greasefree bowl until soft peaks form. Fold the whites into the chocolate mixture. Pour into the prepared loaf tin and freeze overnight.

To serve, remove the terrine from the freezer about 10–15 minutes before serving. Turn out of the tin and cut into slices. Serve with fruit coulis and strawberries.

2 tbsp granulated sugar
5 tbsp water
300 g/10$\frac{1}{2}$ oz white chocolate
3 eggs, separated
300 ml/10 fl oz double cream

TO SERVE
fruit coulis
fresh strawberries

Chocolate & Orange Slices

SERVES 8

Lightly grease a 450-g/1-lb loaf tin and line it with clingfilm. Put the chocolate in a heatproof bowl set over a saucepan of gently simmering water. Stir over a low heat until melted. Remove from the heat and leave to cool slightly.

Meanwhile, peel the oranges, removing all traces of pith. Cut the zest into very thin strips. Beat the egg yolks into the chocolate, one at a time, then add most of the orange zest (reserving the rest for decoration), and all the crème fraîche and raisins, and beat until thoroughly combined. Spoon the mixture into the prepared tin, cover with clingfilm and chill for 3–4 hours, until set.

To serve, remove the tin from the refrigerator and turn out the chocolate mould. Remove the clingfilm and cut the mould into slices. Place a slice on individual serving plates and add whipped cream to serve. Decorate with the remaining orange zest.

2 tsp butter, for greasing

450 g/1 lb plain chocolate, broken into pieces

3 small, loose-skinned oranges, such as tangerines, mandarins or satsumas

4 egg yolks

200 ml/7 fl oz crème fraîche

2 tbsp raisins

300 ml/10 fl oz whipped cream, to serve

Cherry & Chocolate Meringue

SERVES 4

Preheat the oven to 140°C/275°F/Gas Mark 1. Line a baking sheet with greaseproof paper.

Whisk the egg whites until stiff. Gradually add the sugar, and whisk until stiff and shiny. Fold in the cornflour, vinegar, cocoa and chocolate. Spread the meringue on to the baking sheet to form a 24-cm/9¹/2-inch disc. Bake for 1¹/2 hours.

Turn off the oven and leave the meringue in the oven for 45 minutes.

To make the topping, whisk the cream and icing sugar until stiff, then chill. Cut the cherries in half and remove the stones, but keep a few whole. Melt the maple syrup with the butter in a frying pan and stir in the stoned cherries to coat, then set aside to cool.

To serve, peel off the paper from the cool meringue and put the meringue on to a dish. Spoon the cream into the centre and pile on the cherries, using the whole ones around the edge. Top with the caraque.

4 large egg whites
200 g/7 oz caster sugar
1 tsp cornflour, sifted
1 tsp white wine vinegar
1 tbsp cocoa powder
140 g/5 oz plain chocolate,
   chopped

TOPPING
400 ml/14 fl oz double cream
25 g/1 oz icing sugar, sifted
450 g/1 lb black cherries
4 tbsp maple syrup
4 tbsp unsalted butter
plain chocolate caraque,
   to decorate

Chocolate Trifle

SERVES 8

Cut the cake into slices and make 'sandwiches' with the raspberry jam. Cut the 'sandwiches' into cubes and place in a large glass serving bowl. Sprinkle with amaretto. Spread the fruit over the cake.

To make the custard, put the egg yolks and sugar in a bowl and whisk until thick and pale. Stir in the cornflour. Put the milk in a saucepan and heat until almost boiling. Pour on to the yolk mixture, stirring. Return the mixture to the saucepan and bring just to the boil, stirring constantly until it thickens. Remove from the heat and leave to cool slightly. Put the chocolate in a bowl set over a saucepan of simmering water until melted, then add to the custard. Pour over the cake and fruit. Cool, cover and chill for 2 hours to set.

Put the cream in a bowl and whip until soft peaks form. Beat in the sugar and vanilla. Spoon over the trifle. Decorate with truffles and chocolate shapes and then chill until ready to serve.

280 g/10 oz ready-made
    chocolate loaf cake
3–4 tbsp seedless raspberry jam
4 tbsp amaretto
250 g/9 oz packet frozen
    mixed red fruit, thawed

CHOCOLATE CUSTARD
6 egg yolks
55 g/2 oz caster sugar
1 tbsp cornflour
500 ml/18 fl oz milk
55 g/2 oz dark chocolate,
    broken into pieces

TOPPING
225 ml/8 fl oz double cream
1 tbsp caster sugar
$\frac{1}{2}$ tsp vanilla essence

TO DECORATE
ready-made chocolate truffles
chocolate shapes

Chocolate & Vanilla Creams

MAKES 4

Place the cream and sugar in a saucepan and add the vanilla pod. Heat gently, stirring until the sugar has dissolved, then bring to the boil. Reduce the heat and simmer for 2–3 minutes.

Remove the saucepan from the heat and take out the vanilla pod. Stir in the crème fraîche.

Sprinkle the gelatine over the water in a small heatproof bowl and let it go spongy, then set over a saucepan of hot water and stir until dissolved. Stir into the cream mixture. Pour half of this mixture into another mixing bowl.

Put the plain chocolate in a heatproof bowl over a saucepan of simmering water until melted. Stir the melted chocolate into one half of the cream mixture. Pour the chocolate mixture into 4 individual glasses or glass serving dishes and chill for 15–20 minutes, until just set. While the chocolate mixture is chilling, keep the vanilla mixture at room temperature.

Spoon the vanilla mixture on top of the chocolate mixture and chill until the vanilla cream is set. When ready to serve, decorate with the chopped caraque.

450 ml/16 fl oz double cream
6 tbsp caster sugar
1 vanilla pod
200 ml/7 fl oz crème fraîche
2 tsp powdered gelatine
3 tbsp water
50 g/1¾ oz plain chocolate,
 broken into pieces
marbled chocolate caraque,
 chopped, to decorate

Chocolate Milk Shakes

SERVES 4

Pour the milk, chocolate syrup and coffee syrup into a food processor or blender and gently process until blended. Add the ice cream and process to a smooth consistency.

Pour into glasses.

To decorate, spoon the cream into a piping bag with a large, star-shaped nozzle. Pipe generous amounts of cream on top of the milk shakes. Dust with the cocoa powder and serve.

300 ml/10 fl oz milk
2 tbsp chocolate syrup
2 tbsp coffee syrup
800 g/1 lb 12 oz chocolate ice
  cream

TO DECORATE
150 ml/5 fl oz double cream,
  whipped
cocoa powder, for dusting

Little Treats & Luxury Drinks

Chocolate Almond Petits Fours

MAKES 16

Preheat the oven to 190°C/375°F/Gas Mark 5. Line a baking tray with greaseproof paper. Put the ground almonds, sugar and cocoa powder in a bowl and mix together well. Add the egg white and mix to form a firm mixture.

Fill a piping bag, fitted with a small plain nozzle, with the mixture and pipe 5-cm/2-inch lengths, spaced well apart, on to the prepared baking tray. Place an almond half on top of each.

Bake in the oven for about 5 minutes, until firm. Transfer to a wire rack and leave to cool.

When the petits fours are cold, melt the chocolate in a heatproof bowl set over a saucepan of gently simmering water. Dip each end of the petits fours into the melted chocolate, then leave on the wire rack to set.

40 g/1½ oz ground almonds
85 g/3 oz granulated sugar
5 tsp cocoa powder
1 egg white
8 blanched almonds, halved
55 g/2 oz plain chocolate, broken
  into pieces

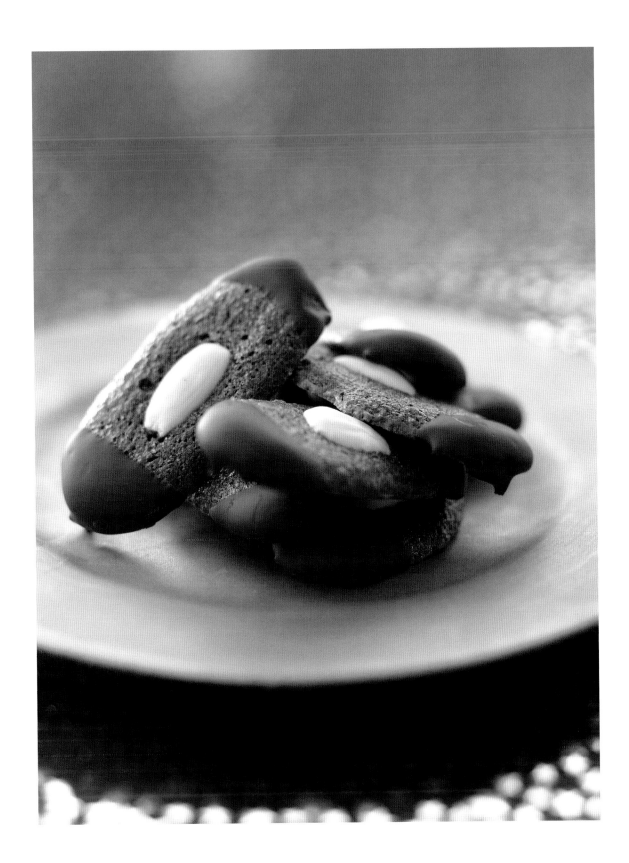

Ginger Chocolate Fudge

MAKES AROUND 50 PIECES

Grease an 18-cm/7-inch square, shallow tin or a 20 x 15-cm/8 x 6-inch rectangular, shallow tin. Dry the syrup off the pieces of stem ginger on kitchen paper, then chop finely.

Pour the milk into a large, heavy-based saucepan and add the chocolate, butter and sugar. Heat gently, stirring all the time, until the chocolate and butter have melted and the sugar has completely dissolved.

Bring to the boil and boil for about 10–15 minutes, stirring occasionally, until a little of the mixture, when dropped into a small bowl of cold water, forms a soft ball when rolled between the fingers.

Remove the saucepan from the heat and stir in the chopped ginger. Leave to cool for 5 minutes, then beat the mixture vigorously with a wooden spoon, until thick, creamy and grainy.

Immediately pour the mixture into the prepared tin, leave to cool, then mark into small squares. Leave the fudge until cold and set, then cut up the squares with a sharp knife.

115 g/4 oz butter, plus extra for greasing
6 pieces stem ginger
300 ml/10 fl oz milk
150 g/5$\frac{1}{2}$ oz plain chocolate, broken into pieces
450 g/1 lb granulated sugar

Fruit & Nut Fudge

MAKES 36 PIECES

Lightly grease a 20-cm/8-inch square cake tin.

Put the chocolate in a heatproof bowl with the butter and evaporated milk and set over a saucepan of gently simmering water. Stir until the chocolate and butter have melted and the mixture is well blended.

Remove the bowl from the heat and gradually beat in the icing sugar. Stir the hazelnuts and sultanas into the mixture. Press the fudge into the prepared tin and smooth the top. Chill until firm.

Tip the fudge out on to a chopping board and cut into squares. Chill in the refrigerator until required.

2 tbsp butter, plus extra for
  greasing
250 g/9 oz plain chocolate,
  broken into pieces
4 tbsp evaporated milk
450 g/1 lb icing sugar, sifted
50 g/1¾ oz roughly chopped
  hazelnuts
50 g/1¾ oz sultanas

Chocolate Creams

MAKES ABOUT 30

Line a baking tray with greaseproof paper. Melt 55 g/2 oz of the chocolate in a large heatproof bowl set over a saucepan of gently simmering water. Stir in the cream and remove the bowl from the heat.

Sift the icing sugar into the melted chocolate then, using a fork, mix together well. Knead to form a firm, smooth, pliable mixture.

Lightly dust a work surface with drinking chocolate powder, turn out the mixture, and roll out to a 5-mm/^{1}/$_4$-inch thickness, then cut into rounds, using a 2.5-cm/1-inch plain round cutter.

Transfer to the prepared baking tray and leave to stand for about 12 hours, or overnight, until set and dry.

When the chocolate creams have set, line a baking tray with greaseproof paper. Melt the remaining chocolate in a heatproof bowl set over a saucepan of gently simmering water. Using 2 forks, carefully dip each chocolate cream into the melted chocolate. Lift it out quickly, letting any excess chocolate drain against the side of the bowl, and place on the prepared baking tray. Leave to set.

200 g/7 oz plain chocolate, broken into pieces
2 tbsp single cream
225 g/8 oz icing sugar
cocoa powder, for dusting

Nutty Chocolate Clusters

MAKES 30

Line a baking tray with a sheet of greaseproof paper. Put the white chocolate in a large heatproof bowl set over a saucepan of gently simmering water and stir until melted.

Break the digestive biscuits into small pieces. Stir the crumbs into the melted chocolate with the chopped nuts, and stem ginger if using.

Place heaped teaspoons of the mixture on the prepared baking tray.

Chill the mixture until set, then remove from the greaseproof paper.

Melt the plain chocolate as above and let it cool slightly. Dip the clusters into the melted chocolate, allowing the excess to drip back into the bowl. Return the clusters to the baking tray and chill in the refrigerator until set.

175 g/6 oz white chocolate, broken into pieces
100 g/3^1/$_2$ oz digestive biscuits
100 g/3^1/$_2$ oz chopped macadamia nuts or Brazil nuts
25 g/1 oz stem ginger, chopped (optional)
175 g/6 oz plain chocolate, broken into pieces

Mini Florentines

MAKES 40

Preheat the oven to 180°C/350°F/Gas Mark 4. Grease and flour 2 baking trays or line with greaseproof paper.

Place the butter in a small saucepan and heat gently until melted. Add the sugar, stir until dissolved, then bring the mixture to the boil. Remove from the heat and stir in the sultanas, cherries, ginger, sunflower seeds and almonds. Mix well, then beat in the cream.

Place small teaspoons of the fruit and nut mixture on to the prepared baking trays, allowing plenty of room for the mixture to spread during baking. Bake in the preheated oven for 10–12 minutes, or until light golden in colour.

Remove from the oven and, while still hot, use a circular biscuit cutter to pull in the edges to form perfect circles. Leave to cool and go crisp before removing from the baking trays.

Put the chocolate in a heatproof bowl set over a saucepan of gently simmering water and stir until melted. Spread most of the chocolate on to a sheet of greaseproof paper. When the chocolate is on the point of setting, place the biscuits flat-side down on the chocolate and let it harden completely.

Cut around the florentines and remove from the greaseproof paper. Spread a little more chocolate on the coated side of the florentines and use a fork to mark waves in the chocolate. Leave to set. Keep cool.

6 tbsp butter, plus extra for
    greasing
plain flour, for dusting
75 g/2¾ oz caster sugar
2 tbsp sultanas or raisins
2 tbsp chopped glacé cherries
2 tbsp chopped stem ginger
25 g/1 oz sunflower seeds
100 g/3½ oz flaked almonds
2 tbsp double cream
175 g/6 oz plain or milk
    chocolate, broken into pieces

Hot Chocolate Cherries

SERVES 4

Put the water, sugar and lemon rind into a heavy-based saucepan and bring to the boil over a low heat, stirring constantly until the sugar has dissolved. Add the cherries and cook, stirring constantly, for 1 minute. Remove the saucepan from the heat and, using a slotted spoon, transfer the cherries to a flameproof dish. Reserve the syrup.

Preheat the grill to medium. Put the cocoa powder in a bowl and mix in a pinch of salt. Whisking constantly, pour in the cream in a steady stream. Remove and discard the lemon rind from the syrup, then stir in the cream mixture. Return the pan to the heat and bring to the boil, stirring constantly. Simmer over a very low heat, stirring occasionally, for 10–15 minutes, or until reduced by about half.

Remove from the heat, stir in the maraschino liqueur and pour the sauce over the cherries. Place under the preheated grill for 2 minutes, then serve.

4 tbsp water
55 g/2 oz caster sugar
1 strip pared lemon rind
450 g/1 lb sweet black cherries, stoned
1 tbsp cocoa powder
salt
4 tbsp double cream
4 tbsp maraschino liqueur or cherry brandy

White Chocolate Truffles

MAKES 20

Line a Swiss roll tin with greaseproof paper.

Place the butter and cream in a small saucepan and bring slowly to the boil, stirring constantly. Boil for 1 minute, then remove from the heat.

Add the chocolate to the cream. Stir until melted, then beat in the liqueur if using.

Pour into the prepared tin and chill for about 2 hours until firm.

Break off pieces of the mixture and roll them into balls. Chill for an additional 30 minutes before finishing the truffles.

To finish, put the white chocolate in a heatproof bowl set over a saucepan of gently simmering water until melted. Dip the balls in the chocolate, letting the excess drip back into the bowl. Place on non-stick baking paper, swirl the chocolate with the tines of a fork, and let it harden.

2 tbsp unsalted butter
5 tbsp double cream
225 g/8 oz good-quality
  Swiss white chocolate, broken
  into pieces
1 tbsp orange liqueur (optional)
100 g/3½ oz white chocolate,
  broken into pieces, for coating

Italian Chocolate Truffles

MAKES 24

Melt the plain chocolate with the amaretto or orange liqueur in a heatproof bowl set over a saucepan of gently simmering water, stirring until well combined.

Add the butter and stir until it has melted. Stir in the icing sugar and the ground almonds.

Leave the mixture in a cool place until firm enough to roll into 24 balls.

Place the grated chocolate on a plate and roll the truffles in the chocolate to coat them.

Place the truffles in paper sweet cases and chill.

175 g/6 oz plain chocolate, broken into pieces
2 tbsp amaretto or orange liqueur
3 tbsp unsalted butter
4 tbsp icing sugar
50 g/1¾ oz ground almonds
50 g/1¾ oz grated chocolate

Chocolate Liqueurs

MAKES 40

Line a baking tray with a sheet of greaseproof paper. Put the plain chocolate in a heatproof bowl and set over a saucepan of gently simmering water. Stir until melted. Spoon the chocolate into 40 paper sweet cases, spreading up the sides with a spoon or brush. Place upside down on the baking tray and leave to set.

Carefully peel away the paper cases. Place a cherry or nut in each cup.

To make the filling, place the double cream in a mixing bowl and sift the icing sugar on top. Whisk the cream until it is just holding its shape, then whisk in the liqueur.

Place the cream in a piping bag fitted with a 1-cm/½-inch plain nozzle and pipe a little into each chocolate case. Leave to chill for 20 minutes.

To decorate, spoon the plain chocolate over the cream to cover it. Add the caraque and let it harden.

100 g/3½ oz plain chocolate,
  broken into pieces
20 glacé cherries
20 hazelnuts or macadamia nuts
150 ml/5 fl oz double cream
2 tbsp icing sugar
4 tbsp liqueur

TO DECORATE
50 g/1¾ oz plain chocolate,
  melted
marbled chocolate caraque

Rum & Chocolate Cups

MAKES 12

To make the chocolate cups, place the chocolate in a heatproof bowl set over a saucepan of gently simmering water. Stir over a low heat until the chocolate is just melted but not too runny, then remove from the heat. Spoon about $^1/_2$ teaspoon of melted chocolate into a foil sweet case and brush it over the base and up the sides. Coat 11 more foil cases in the same way and leave to set for 30 minutes. Chill in the refrigerator for 15 minutes. If necessary, reheat the chocolate in the heatproof bowl to melt it again, then coat the foil cases with a second, slightly thinner coating. Let the cases chill in the refrigerator for an additional 30 minutes.

Meanwhile, make the filling. Place the chocolate in a heatproof bowl set over a saucepan of gently simmering water. Stir over a low heat until melted, then remove from the heat. Leave to cool slightly, then stir in the rum and beat in the mascarpone cheese until fully incorporated and smooth. Leave to cool completely, stirring occasionally.

Spoon the filling into a piping bag fitted with a 1-cm/$^1/_2$-inch star nozzle. If preferred, carefully peel away the foil cases from the chocolate cups. Pipe the filling into the cups and top each one with a toasted hazelnut.

55 g/2 oz plain chocolate, broken into pieces
12 toasted hazelnuts

FILLING
115 g/4 oz plain chocolate, broken into pieces
1 tbsp dark rum
4 tbsp mascarpone cheese

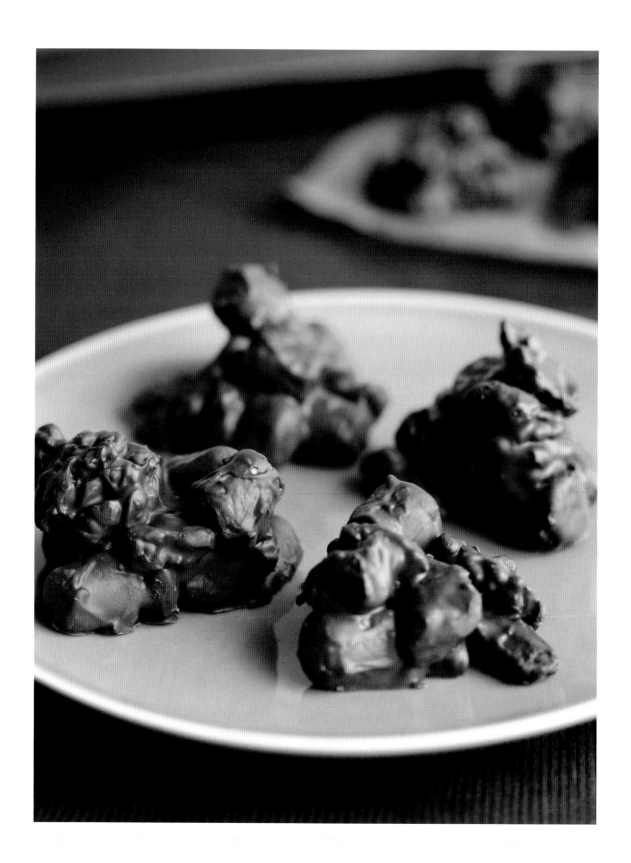

Rocky Road Bites

MAKES 18

Line a baking tray with greaseproof paper and set aside.

Put the milk chocolate in a large heatproof bowl. Set the bowl over a saucepan of gently simmering water and stir until the chocolate has melted.

Stir in the marshmallows, walnuts and apricots, and toss in the melted chocolate until well covered.

Put heaped teaspoonfuls of the mixture on the prepared baking tray.

Let the sweets chill in the refrigerator until set.

Once set, carefully remove the sweets from the greaseproof paper.

Place in paper sweet cases to serve, if desired.

125 g/4^1/$_2$ oz milk chocolate, broken into pieces

40 g/1^1/$_2$ oz mini multi-coloured marshmallows

25 g/1 oz chopped walnuts

25 g/1 oz ready-to-eat dried apricots, chopped

Apricot & Almond Clusters

MAKES 24–28

Put the chocolate and honey in a heatproof bowl set over a saucepan of gently simmering water and stir until melted and smooth.

Stir in the apricots and almonds.

Drop teaspoonfuls of the mixture into paper sweet cases. Leave to set.

115 g/4 oz plain chocolate, broken into pieces
2 tbsp clear honey
115 g/4 oz ready-to-eat dried apricots, chopped
55 g/2 oz blanched almonds, chopped

Brazil Nut Brittle

MAKES 20

Brush the bottom of a 20-cm/8-inch square cake tin with oil and line with greaseproof paper. Put half the plain chocolate in a heatproof bowl and set over a saucepan of gently simmering water. Stir until melted, then spread in the prepared tin.

Sprinkle with the chopped Brazil nuts, white chocolate and fudge. Melt the remaining plain chocolate pieces and pour over the top.

Let the brittle set, then break up into jagged pieces using the tip of a strong knife.

sunflower oil, for brushing

350 g/12 oz plain chocolate, broken into pieces

100 g/3^{1}/$_{2}$ oz shelled Brazil nuts, chopped

175 g/6 oz white chocolate, roughly chopped

175 g/6 oz fudge, roughly chopped

Chocolate Fondue

SERVES 6

Using a sharp knife, peel and core the pineapple, then cut the flesh into cubes. Peel the mango and cut the flesh into cubes. Peel back the papery outer skin of the physalis and twist at the top to make a 'handle'. Arrange all the fruit on 6 serving plates and leave to chill in the refrigerator.

To make the fondue, place the chocolate and cream in a fondue pot. Heat gently, stirring constantly, until the chocolate has melted. Stir in the brandy until thoroughly blended and the chocolate mixture is smooth.

Place the fondue pot over the burner to keep warm. To serve, allow each guest to dip the fruit into the sauce, using fondue forks or bamboo skewers.

1 pineapple
1 mango
12 physalis
250 g/9 oz fresh strawberries
250 g/9 oz seedless green
  grapes

FONDUE
250 g/9 oz plain chocolate,
  broken into pieces
150 ml/5 fl oz double cream
2 tbsp brandy

French Chocolate Sauce

SERVES 2–4

Bring the cream gently to the boil in a small, heavy-based saucepan over a low heat. Remove the saucepan from the heat, add the broken chocolate and stir until smooth.

Stir in the liqueur and serve immediately, or keep the sauce warm until required. Serve over ice cream.

6 tbsp double cream

85 g/3 oz dark chocolate, broken into small pieces

2 tbsp orange liqueur

ice cream, to serve

Chocolate Fudge Sauce

SERVES 2–4

Pour the cream into the top of a double boiler or a heatproof bowl set over a saucepan of gently simmering water. Add the butter and sugar and stir until the mixture is smooth. Remove from the heat.

Stir in the chocolate, a few pieces at a time, waiting until each batch has melted before adding the next. Add the brandy and stir the sauce until smooth. Cool to room temperature before serving.

150 ml/5 fl oz double cream
4 tbsp butter, cut into small
    pieces
3 tbsp caster sugar
175 g/6 oz white chocolate,
    broken into pieces
2 tbsp brandy

Real Hot Chocolate

SERVES 1–2

Place the chocolate in a large, heatproof jug. Place the milk in a heavy-based saucepan and bring to the boil. Pour about one-quarter of the milk on to the chocolate and leave until the chocolate has softened.

Whisk the milk and chocolate mixture until smooth. Return the remaining milk to the heat and return to the boil, then pour on to the chocolate, whisking constantly.

Pour into warmed mugs or cups and decorate with chocolate curls. Serve immediately.

40 g/1½ oz plain chocolate,
  broken into pieces
300 ml/10 fl oz milk
chocolate curls, to decorate

Hot Chocolate Float

SERVES 4

Pour the milk into a saucepan. Break the chocolate into small pieces and add to the saucepan with the sugar. Stir over a low heat until the chocolate has melted, the sugar has dissolved and the mixture is smooth. Remove the saucepan from the heat.

Put 1 scoop of coconut ice cream into each of 4 heatproof glasses, top with a scoop of chocolate ice cream, then repeat the layers.

Pour the chocolate-flavoured milk into the glasses, top with whipped cream and serve immediately.

450 ml/16 fl oz milk

225 g/8 oz plain chocolate

2 tbsp caster sugar

8 scoops coconut ice cream

8 scoops plain chocolate ice cream

whipped cream, to decorate

Cinnamon Mocha

SERVES 6

Put the chocolate in a large heatproof bowl set over a saucepan of gently simmering water. Add the cream and stir until the chocolate has melted and the mixture is smooth.

Pour in the coffee, add the cinnamon, and whisk until foamy. If serving hot, pour into heatproof glasses or mugs, top with cream and caraque, and serve immediately. If serving cold, remove the bowl from the heat and leave to cool, chill in the refrigerator until required, then decorate with whipped cream, a sprinkling of ground cinnamon, and the caraque.

250 g/9 oz milk chocolate, broken into pieces

175 ml/6 fl oz single cream

1 litre/1¾ pints freshly brewed coffee

1 tsp ground cinnamon, plus extra to decorate

TO DECORATE

whipped cream

marbled chocolate caraque

Marshmallow Float

SERVES 4

Finely chop the chocolate with a knife or in a food processor. Do not over-process or the chocolate will melt.

Pour the milk into a saucepan and bring to just below boiling point. Remove the saucepan from the heat and whisk in the sugar and the chocolate.

Pour into warmed mugs or heatproof glasses, top with marshmallows and serve immediately.

225 g/8 oz plain chocolate,
    broken into pieces
900 ml/1$\frac{1}{2}$ pints milk
3 tbsp caster sugar
8 marshmallows

INDEX

almonds
almond & hazelnut gâteau 29
apricot & almond clusters 206
chocolate almond petits fours 182
chocolate cake with syrup 18
chocolate fudge cake 12
chocolate madeira cake 26
chocolate orange muffins 59
chocolate praline ice cream 138
crispy chocolate pie 44
Italian chocolate truffles 199
ladies' kisses 132
marble cake 20
mini florentines 193
rippled chocolate gâteau 23

apricots
apricot & almond clusters 206
rocky road bites 205

bars & slices
chocolate caramel squares 129
chocolate chip flapjacks 130
chocolate peanut butter slices 118
chocolate pistachio bars 126

berries
blackberry chocolate flan 36
chocolate blueberry tarts 47
chocolate trifle 166
raspberry chocolate boxes 174

biscuits see cookies

Brazil nuts
Brazil nut brittle 208
chocolate chiffon pie 35
chocolate temptations 123
white chocolate cookies 112

brownies
black Russian brownies 80
chocolate brownies 68
chocolate fudge brownies 72
double chocolate brownies with fudge
    sauce 71
marbled chocolate cheesecake
    brownies 78
sticky chocolate brownies 74
white chocolate brownies 77

cakes
almond & hazelnut gâteau 29
Black Forest roulade 42
chocolate cake with syrup 18
chocolate fudge cake 12
chocolate ganache cake 14
chocolate madeira cake 26
chocolate truffle torte 17
marble cake 20
mocha layer cake 24
rippled chocolate gâteau 23
see also cupcakes

cherries
Black Forest roulade 42
cherry & chocolate meringue 160
chocolate queen of puddings 50
chocolate liqueurs 200
hot chocolate cherries 194
mini florentines 193

coffee
cappuccino soufflé puddings 48
chocolate cake with syrup 18
chocolate milk shakes 178
chocolate temptations 123
chocolate truffle torte 17
cinnamon mocha 220
marble cake 20
mocha cupcakes with whipped cream 95
mocha layer cake 24
mocha muffins 65
mocha walnut cookies 117
raspberry chocolate boxes 174
tiramisù layers 153

cookies
chocolate chip oaties 100
chocolate & coffee wholemeal 114
chocolate orange 106
chocolate temptations 123
chocolate wheatmeals 120
cookies & cream sandwiches 111
double chocolate chip 102
ladies' kisses 132
mocha walnut 117
nutty drizzles 108
white chocolate 112
zebra cookies 105
see also bars & slices

cream cheese
brownie bottom cheesecake 165
chocolate cupcakes with cream
    cheese icing 89
chocolate fudge brownies 72
chocolate mint swirls 171
chocolate orange muffins 59
deep chocolate cheesecake 162
marbled chocolate cheesecake brownies 78
rum & chocolate cups 202
tiramisù layers 153

cupcakes
chocolate butterfly cakes 83
chocolate chip cupcakes 86
chocolate cupcakes with cream cheese
    icing 89
dark & white fudge cupcakes 84
devil's food cakes with chocolate frosting 92
mocha cupcakes with whipped cream 95
tiny chocolate cupcakes with ganache
    icing 96
warm molten-centred chocolate
    cupcakes 90

dessert sauces
chocolate fudge sauce 214
French chocolate sauce 212

desserts, cold
brownie bottom cheesecake 165
cherry & chocolate meringue 160
chocolate hazelnut parfaits 159
chocolate mint swirls 171
chocolate & orange slices 156
chocolate rum pots 168
chocolate trifle 166
chocolate & vanilla creams 172
deep chocolate cheesecake 162

raspberry chocolate boxes 174
rich chocolate mousses 150
tiramisù layers 153
white chocolate terrine 154
see also ice cream

desserts, hot
cappuccino soufflé puddings 48
chocolate fondue 211
chocolate queen of puddings 50

drinks
chocolate milk shakes 178
cinnamon mocha 220
cool minty chocolate 177
hot chocolate float 218
marshmallow float 223
real hot chocolate 217

flans, pies & tarts
blackberry chocolate flan 36
chocolate blueberry tarts 47
chocolate chiffon pie 35
chocolate crumble pie 32
chocolate mousse tart 41
crispy chocolate pie 44
Mississippi mud pie 30
toffee chocolate puff tarts 38

florentines, mini 193

ginger
ginger chocolate fudge 184
mini florentines 193
nutty chocolate clusters 190

hazelnuts
almond & hazelnut gâteau 29
chocolate brownies 68
chocolate & coffee wholemeal cookies 114
chocolate hazelnut parfaits 159
chocolate temptations 123
fruit & nut fudge 187
rum & chocolate cups 202

ice cream
chocolate chip, with hot chocolate
    fudge sauce 136
chocolate ice cream bites 148
chocolate ice cream bombe 147
chocolate ice cream roll 144
chocolate peppermint crisp terrine 142
chocolate praline 138
cool minty chocolate 177
hot chocolate float 218
white & dark chocolate 141

marshmallows
marshmallow float 223
marshmallow muffins 66
rocky road bites 205

mint
chocolate mint swirls 171
chocolate peppermint crisp terrine 142
cool minty chocolate 177

muffins
chocolate chip 56
chocolate orange 59

double chocolate 54
marshmallow 66
mocha 65
spiced chocolate 60
triple chocolate 62

nuts
chocolate peanut butter slices 118
chocolate pistachio bars 126
chocolate liqueurs 200
nutty chocolate clusters 190
nutty drizzles 108
see also almonds; Brazil nuts;
    hazelnuts; pecan nuts; walnuts

oats
chocolate & coffee wholemeal cookies 114
chocolate caramel squares 129
chocolate chip flapjacks 130
chocolate chip oaties 100
chocolate peanut butter slices 118
nutty drizzles 108

oranges
chocolate orange cookies 106
chocolate orange muffins 59
chocolate & orange slices 156
deep chocolate cheesecake 162

pecan nuts
chocolate crumble pie 32
chocolate fudge brownies 72

petit fours, chocolate almond 182

raisins & sultanas
chocolate brownies 68
chocolate chip flapjacks 130
chocolate & orange slices 156
fruit & nut fudge 187
mini florentines 193
mocha muffins 65
nutty drizzles 108

scones, chocolate 124

sweets
apricot & almond clusters 206
Brazil nut brittle 208
chocolate creams 188
chocolate liqueurs 200
fruit & nut fudge 187
ginger chocolate fudge 184
nutty chocolate clusters 190
rocky road bites 205
rum & chocolate cups 202
see also truffles

toffee chocolate puff tarts 38

truffles
Italian chocolate 199
white chocolate 196

walnuts
black Russian brownies 80
mocha walnut cookies 117
rocky road bites 205
white chocolate brownies 77